ANTS

Robbie Byerly

eyes

Look at the ant with the eyes.

wings

Look at the ant with the wings.

legs

Look at the ant with the legs.

egg

Look at the ant with the egg.

flower

Look at the ant with the flower.

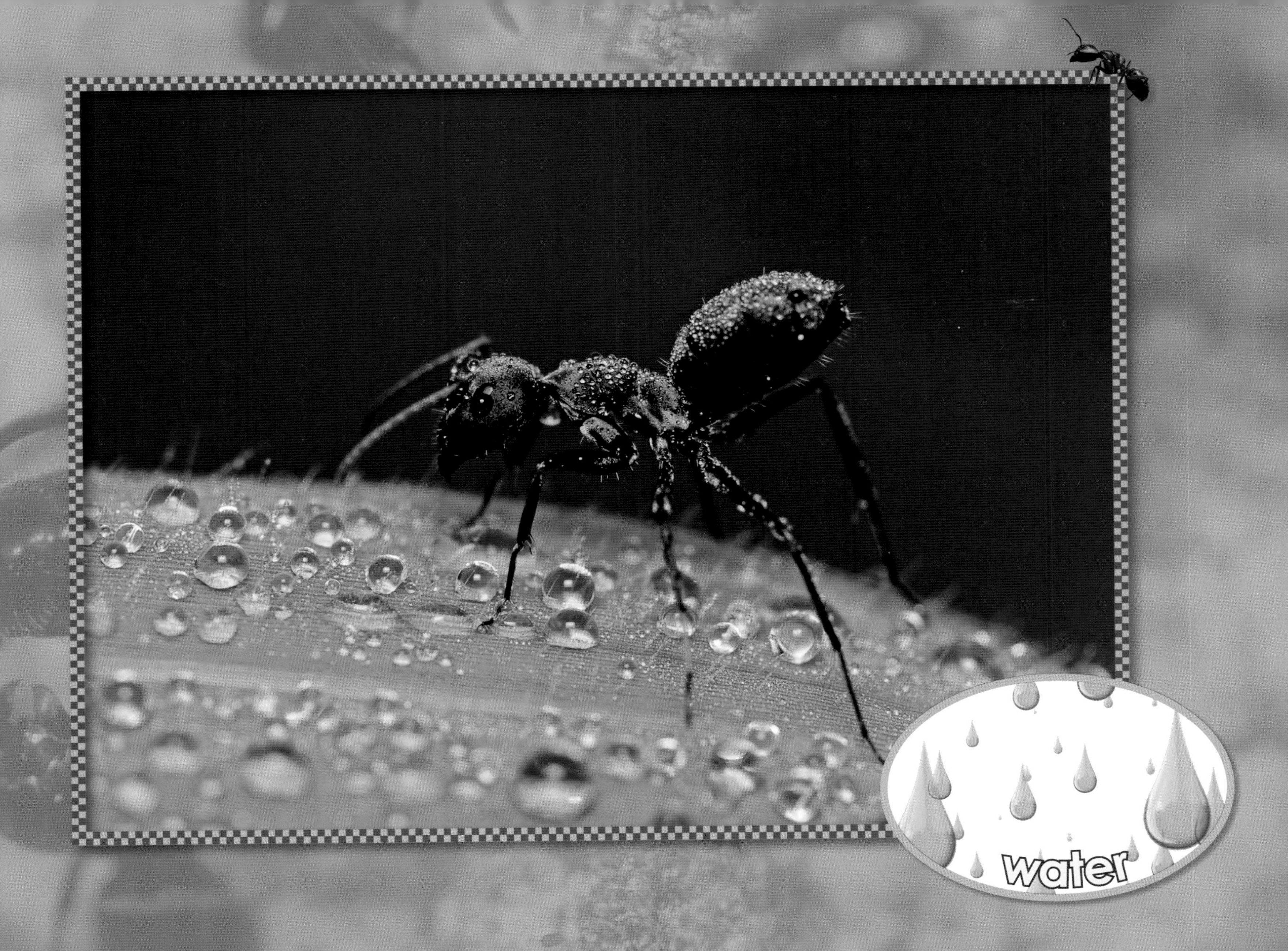
water

Look at the ant with the water.

leaf

Look at the ant with the leaf.

grasshopper

Look at the ant with the grasshopper.

ladybug

Look at the ant with the ladybug.

bee

Look at the ant with the bee.

fly

Look at the ant with the fly.

caterpillar

Look at the ant with the caterpillar.

spider

Look at the ant with the spider.

lizard

Look at the ant with the lizard.

Power Words

Look
look
at
the
with